W9-CBE-018

THE GOVERNMENT MANUAL™ FOR NEW SUPERHEROES

THE GOVERNMENT MANUAL FOR NEW SUPERHEROES

MATTHEW DAVID BROZIK
AND
JACOB SAGER WEINSTEIN

Andrews McMeel
Publishing

Kansas City

ISBN-13: 978-0-7407-5462-3

ISBN-10: 0-7407-5462-9

05 06 07 08 09 MLT 10 9 8 7 6 5 4 3 2

Library of Congress Control Number: 2005924763

www.andrewsmcmeel.com

Dedication

As an impartial bureaucratic entity, the Government cannot feel abiding love, but if it could, it would surely dedicate this work to the honor of Lauren Sager Weinstein and to the memory of Aaron Shansky.

Acknowledgments

The Government offers its top-level gratitude to the following for their efforts on behalf of this vitally important work:

Robert Shepard (a/k/a THE AGENT);

Lane Butler (a/k/a EDITRIX: DELETER OF COMMAS); and

Jake Barnes, Richard Herschlag, Rob Kutner, Glen McGorty, Stuart Rosen, Lucinda Shih, and **W. Brad Waller** (collectively known as FIRST READERS OF JUSTICE).

The Government thanks also a mysterious and shadowy organization known only as THE AMALGAMATED ALLIANCE OF PARENTS, SIBLINGS, AND GRANDPARENTS, LOCAL 8 for numerous contributions that may not be identified without compromising national security.

Contents

Memorandum

THE GOVERNMENT
DEPARTMENT OF JUSTICE
BUREAU OF SUPERHEROICS

TO: All Aspirants to Superhero Status
FROM: Dr. Jane Loudermilk, Undersecretary of
         Superheroics
RE: "The Government Manual for New Superheroes"

Your Government wants you to succeed in whatever you
choose to do (except if you choose to overthrow the
Government). To this end, the Government publishes a
series of guides to provide Useful Information, such
as "The Government Manual for New Homeowners" and
"The Government Manual for New Motor Vehicle
Operators" (but *not* "The Government Manual for New
Overthrowers of the Government").

"The Government Manual for New Superheroes" will
help you get started as a costumed crimefighter.
Because it is meant to aid the broadest possible
audience, it has been written for those who do not
have superpowers. That is, it is intended mostly for
the moody millionaire industrialists, the crusading
reporters, and the chipper young orphans who,

according to the latest census figures, make up the larger part of the populace. It is less helpful for the aliens, psychic prodigies, mythic gods, and mysterious dwellers of unseen realms who make up the rest.

Herein you will find Indispensable Guidance regarding the many and varied options you must consider and actions you must take early on. A superhero cannot be a fence-sitter, after all. Even the late, legendary FENCESITTER took action from time to time, albeit often in an untimely fashion.

At the outset of your career arise some of the most difficult but potentially rewarding choices you will ever need to make: your name, first and foremost. Will mention of your moniker give your foes fits, or giggles? Next: your costume—if you are going to be in the same outfit every time duty calls, you had best pick one that is both comfortable and practical, and flattering as well. Your symbol? An icon is worth a thousand catchphrases, and yours will stand for what you stand for. Where will you hide out? In whom will you confide? Will you go solo or do you prefer company, either in the form of a protégé (or "sidekick," in Government-sanctioned parlance) or teammates of equal stature, if different skills? And when you are finally ready to declare yourself super, when you have completed the proper forms and paid your registration fees and union dues, whom will you fight?

This guide is written in Straightforward Language—the kind of simple, casual speech you might use every day as you indulge in lengthy interior monologues that explain your origins, your current mental state, and any previous encounters you might have had with the persons around you. Numerous headings divide the material into Discrete Sections, and words have been capitalized only when Strictly Necessary. The overall presentation in printed and bound form allows you to use a bookmark to hold your place if you need to stop reading in order to, say, render assistance to a fellow citizen, or take something off the stove. Topics and asides of especial noteworthiness are set apart from the main text in boxes introduced by this symbol:

That said, you are now only a foreword, eight chapters, one afterword, and two appendices from superheroism. We wish you the speed of MARATHON-MAN, the strength of THE FORTE, and the wisdom of SCHOLARA: THE HUMAN FOOTNOTE as you begin as an up, up, and coming superhero.

Foreword

by THE ELIMINATORIAN

If I had a nickel for every time a young hopeful asked me how to be a superhero, I'd have a million nickels, which I would use to crush my hated enemies beneath a gleaming mountain of coinage, and when they opened their foul mouths to scream, the tiny shimmering discs would flood down their throats, choking the life out of their evildoing bodies like an army of little silver vigilantes.

And that's why I was so glad when the Government told me about this handbook for aspiring crusaders who have yet to don their first costumes. I hope it will help turn youngsters away from such temptations as drinking, gambling, and studying, and toward the really important pursuits of smiting and avenging.

It is with great pleasure, therefore, that I recommend this book to anyone with an interest in socially constructive violence.

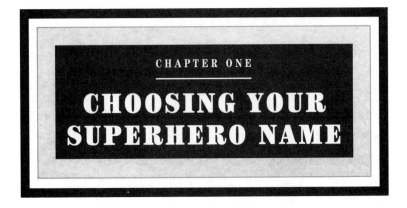

CHAPTER ONE

CHOOSING YOUR SUPERHERO NAME

You have a perfectly ordinary name—rhythmic, alliterative, and perhaps containing a play on words. Until now, you have answered to your name whenever called: at any time of day or night, at home, at work, or at the club. You are about to assume another identity, however, presumably only your second, and this second you will also need a name. Unlike your first—that is, your civilian—name, given to you by your parents or the nuns who found you swaddled at the doorstep of their convent in the forest, your *nom de combattre le crime* is for you to choose. This chapter will help you choose wisely.

Not Answering to Your Civilian Name

You will likely find it difficult enough at first remembering to respond to your superhero name once you have adopted it. Therefore, you must prepare for those times when you will be *someone else*, and to answer to your civilian name would confirm the suspicions of those who would do you ill and compromise the safety of your family, friends, and workaday colleagues. Perhaps even before you choose your superhero name you should begin practicing *not answering* to your civilian name for hours at a stretch—unless you are a teenager, in which case you probably already have some practice not responding to your name, at least when called by adults.

The Four Common Varieties

Superhero names generally come in four varieties:

1. _____ (-)Man/Boy or (-)Woman/Girl;
2. The _____ ;
3. [Honorific] _____ ; and
4. _____ .

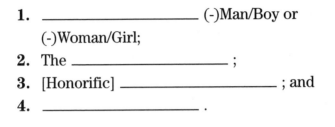

A Word on Hyphenation

If you choose a name of the first common variety, you will be faced with a further dilemma: whether to hyphenate the two halves of your name, leave a space between them, or simply run them together into a single fused moniker. There are those who believe that hyphenation betrays a lack of conviction in one's *super*-iority; leaving a space is tantamount to not becoming a superhero at all. The authors are of the mind that hyphenation or even full separation is wholly a matter of style. That is, "Crumble-Boy" is neither more nor less fearsome than "Crumbleboy" or "Crumble Boy."

And a Word on Adjectives

Another thing to consider if you choose a name of the first flavor, and to a lesser extent if you choose one of the second or third, is the opportunity to inject an adjective, from time to time, as appropriate. For example, if you were THE NEWS, you might also be THE *LOCAL* NEWS. (Additionally, your enemies might appreciate

the opportunity to remark, with contempt,
"Well, well . . . if it isn't yesterday's NEWS.")

A Caution About Honorifics

The appeal of the honorific is the sense of
authority it conveys and the feeling of
accomplishment, even if initially undeserved,
with which it infuses the bearer. The trouble
with an honorific arises when the superhero
using it is called upon to perform the more
mundane tasks commonly associated with the
title.

That is, DOCTOR ELASTIC might be adept at
delivering baddies into the hands of the
authorities, but can he deliver a baby on a stalled
subway train? "Why not?" those on the train
might inquire. "Aren't you DOCTOR ELASTIC?"

What Your Name Should Say About You

Whether you choose to structure your superhero name as a single awe-inspiring or fear-inducing term, alone or with an article, or even with an attached indication of your sex and maturity, your name should suggest, to the greatest extent possible, one of the following:

- The animal, plant, or natural phenomenon you most resemble or admire (e.g., CAPTAIN CHAMOIS, HAIL-GIRL, THE FERN);

- Your exceptional ability or abilities (THE SPEEDREADER, BALANCE BOY);

- The source of your superpowers, if you in fact have superpowers (WHITE NOISE, THE PEWTER FLASK); or

- That you are in general better than non-superheroes (MORE MAN, THE EXEMPLAR, TRUMP).

The Epithet:
An Extra Bit of Bluster

Akin to the introductory adjective, but providing even more of an opportunity for puffery, is the full-blown epithet: the phrase that follows. Will you be DUNE, or DUNE: THE BOY OF SAND?

SHE-MAN or SHE-MAN: PERSON OF POWER?

The choice belongs to You: Reader of This Book.

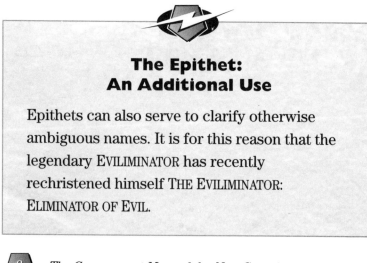

The Epithet:
An Additional Use

Epithets can also serve to clarify otherwise ambiguous names. It is for this reason that the legendary EVILIMINATOR has recently rechristened himself THE EVILIMINATOR: ELIMINATOR OF EVIL.

Rule: First Originated, First Named

There are an unlimited number of names available to the limited number of superheroes active at any given moment, yet certain names are more superheroic than others and are,

"Now it's official: I'm THE LEMONADER!"

therefore, more desirable. Recognizing the need for a free and efficient exchange of information regarding superhero names worldwide, the Unified Nations has established the Superhero Name Registry and Clearinghouse. This august body maintains records of all superheroes around the globe, including dates of origin and adoption of name.

For a nominal fee, the Registry will perform a comprehensive search of its database to determine the availability of any superhero name. Once registered, a superhero name enjoys exclusive ownership by the registrant until the occurrence of certain terminating events, including death of the hero, voluntary surrender of one's name, or documented change of permanent residence to an alternate universe.

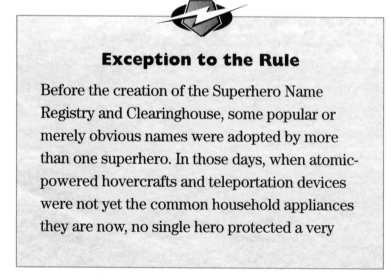

Exception to the Rule

Before the creation of the Superhero Name Registry and Clearinghouse, some popular or merely obvious names were adopted by more than one superhero. In those days, when atomic-powered hovercrafts and teleportation devices were not yet the common household appliances they are now, no single hero protected a very large geographical expanse, and the likelihood of overlap was negligible. The policy of the dispute resolution arm of the Registry is to permit concurrent uses of identical or substantially similar names if the adoptions were made in good faith before the passage of Unified Nations Resolution K-63 ("A Resolution to Establish a Procedure for the Registration of Superhero Names") and upon a showing that the senior—that is, earlier—adopter of the common name is not likely to be called upon to serve superheroically in the Superhero District of the junior. The senior adopter, however, retains the greater right to the common name in all other Districts.

In the alternative, the Registry also sanctions battles *royale* between claimants and will recognize the superior rights of the victorious combatant to the name in dispute. The loser, until he or she adopts a new name, is known (at least officially) as THE LOSER—unless the name in dispute was, in fact, THE LOSER, in which case the winner is known as THE LOSER and the loser known as MUD.

Demeanor the Better

Some superhero names engender hope: BRIGHT HORIZON; THE ENGENDERER; PROFESSOR HOPE. Others instill fear: THE CASTIGATOR; MULCT-MAN; and SCOURGE. Still others are neutral: SALESGIRL; THE CAPE. Remember that you will be adopting not just a new name but a new persona as well, and although that persona can change over time, you should decide on at least the demeanor you will begin with and choose your name in keeping with that decision.

If you want to be the stalwart, flag-waving, do-gooding type, a name like THE ARTFUL DRAFT DODGER will not fly. If you plan to appear only at night, dress all in black, and bend the rules to breaking in your quest for justice, do not name yourself COMMANDER

BABYPOWDER and expect to cow any but the most
sheepish rogues.

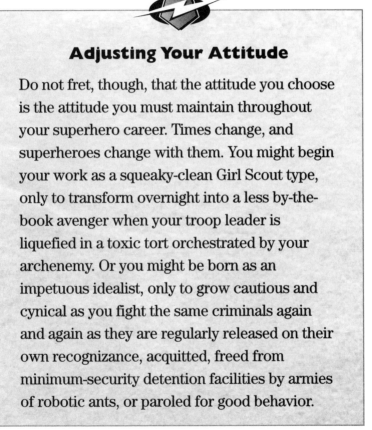

Adjusting Your Attitude

Do not fret, though, that the attitude you choose
is the attitude you must maintain throughout
your superhero career. Times change, and
superheroes change with them. You might begin
your work as a squeaky-clean Girl Scout type,
only to transform overnight into a less by-the-
book avenger when your troop leader is
liquefied in a toxic tort orchestrated by your
archenemy. Or you might be born as an
impetuous idealist, only to grow cautious and
cynical as you fight the same criminals again
and again as they are regularly released on their
own recognizance, acquitted, freed from
minimum-security detention facilities by armies
of robotic ants, or paroled for good behavior.

Keep It Simple, Superhero

"Observe! Overhead in the firmament! There's a waterfowl! There's an aerodyne! There's—"

Will what follows roll off the tongue, or be a mangled mouthful?

MAGIC-MAN does the trick. THE PRESTIDIGITATOR baffles.

THE MOSQUITO has bite. GALLINIPPER is a bloody mess.

Your superhero name will be the harbinger of all of your knowledge, experience, wisdom, and goodwill, but, nonetheless, your name should be terse, concise, brief, pithy. Your appearance, not your appellation, should trip up your enemies. Your title should comfort, not confound, the populace. In short, there is a reason why BIG BANG is remembered to this day, while THE SUPERCONDUCTING NON-COLLOIDAL MEDIUM-ENERGY-BOOSTING SUPERCOLLIDER OF THE GREATER SANDUSKY, OHIO, METROPOLITAN AREA has faded to obscurity.

Remember Which Side You Are On

The inherent *goodness* of good, as opposed to evil, is what made you want to be a superhero in the first place. Your superhero name should remind you, as well as the public, of as much. Therefore, be mindful of the connotation(s) of any name you consider. Though a particular name might seem clever or stylish or "cool," if it suggests bad rather than good, it will work against you. Avoid names like THE EXECRABLE LUNK, COLONEL HURT, and WASTREL.

For the Stranger to This World: Choosing a Human Name

As mentioned at the outset, this manual is primarily intended to aid the otherwise average human born into one of the unenshrouded civilizations of Earth. Nonetheless, the authors include here a brief note regarding the taking of a name for the benefit of the already-super hero for whom a human persona will be an *alter ego*.

The only first names of human males as of this writing are: *John, Jack, Jean, James, Jason, Jacob, Joshua, Justin, Jordan,* and *Jeffrey.*

The only names of females are: *Jan, Jane, Joan, Jeanne, Jenna, Jennifer, Jessica, Julia, Jocelyn,* and *Jacqueline.*

The only surnames are: *Johnson, Jackson, Jameson,; Jacobson, Jefferson, Smith, Jones, Brown, Miller,* and *White.*

L. to r. : Jackie Johnson, Jessica Smith, Jeff Jacobson, Jenna Brown, Jack Miller, Jim Jefferson, and Jeanne White.

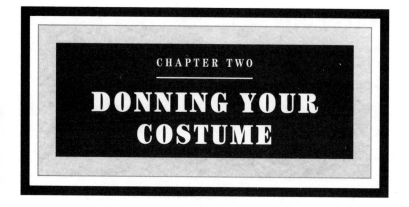

CHAPTER TWO

DONNING YOUR COSTUME

Buyer Beware

No matter what the manufacturer might claim, even the most professionally constructed superhero-themed underpants will make an inadequate costume.

Materials

Prior to the twentieth century, superheroes had available to them for costuming only various woefully inadequate materials. Every schoolchild is familiar with the story of SERGEANT STRIPE, the cotton seams of whose costume burst in 1777, sending one of his silver-dollar buttons flying across the Potomac River only to knock down a cherry tree, with the resulting scandal forcing the man to return permanently to his civilian identity: mild-mannered war hero George Washington.

Fortunately, as a modern-day superhero, you have a nearly limitless range of materials available to you. These may be broken down into two general categories: mysterious substances that are the fruits of your own scientific genius; and Spandex. As a rule, it is best to avoid donning a living costume that is actually an alien parasite, as it will slowly drain your energy until forcibly removed, at which point it will become a vengeance-obsessed, homicidal supervillain. Also, such a costume tends not to be very slimming.

A Table

Substance	Pro	Con
The mysterious fruits of your own scientific genius	Will never rip or get dirty; capable of turning invisible or bursting into flame without damage	You have to be a genius
Spandex	Stretchy	Might cause laughter among today's irony-obsessed, media-savvy youth

A Word on Modesty

It should go without saying that a costume must cover those parts of your body society deems unsuitable for public display. Your goal is to uphold the values of your community, not to test them. However, a costume that is appropriate for one region might be utterly inappropriate for another, as the photographs of topless Amazonian crimefighters that occasionally appear in *National Geographic Magazine of Justice* make plain. If you have plans to combat evil during a vacation abroad, you might consider first paying a visit to that nation's consulate and obtaining a pamphlet on local superhero customs and costumes.

Costume Design

Just because you can shatter concrete blocks with the heel of your foot does not necessarily mean that you can compose an attractive, appropriate ensemble. Unless you are becoming THE COSTUME DESIGNER, your superhero skills likely will lie in areas other than costume design. Don't be ashamed to seek help. There are several reputable, discreet design professionals who charge by the consulting-hour and will keep your identity in the strictest confidence. You might find such a professional by using a powerful spotlight to shine the stark image of a single silver needle against the night sky, or by looking in your local yellow pages.

Whether you work alone or with a designer, you will still need to consider which elements you wish to include in your costume. Some elements are mandatory, while others are optional.

Mandatory

- Your costume must conceal your civilian identity. Some costumes do this through addition (for example, by including a mask); others do it through subtraction (for example, by leaving out the spectacles you usually wear). Whichever approach you take, do not worry about being discovered. Countless scientific studies have shown that the simple act of removing your glasses or of covering the smallest part of your face just around your eyes with the flimsiest of masks can make you appear so completely different that even your most intimate friends will fail to recognize you.

- Your costume should also include boots.

Optional

- If you are a woman, you will need to choose between a costume that reveals large amounts of cleavage and bare skin, and a more modest and demure one that covers you up thoroughly while clinging tightly to every curve of your body.

- For men and women alike, a large, gleaming, metallic belt buckle embellished with your logo is a stylish and tasteful way of letting the world know who you are.

- The most popular optional accessory is, without a doubt, the cape. The cape has certain minor disadvantages: as other experts in the field have noted, it can get caught in the spokes of a passing bicycle, for example, and it might be expensive to dry-clean. However, the simple fact is that nothing says, "Evildoers, beware!" quite like a large piece of cloth tied around your neck.

Some heroes include thick bulletproof armor in their costumes, but this is generally an unpopular choice. It interrupts the sleekness of your profile, ruining your carefully cultivated image of mystery and power. The only thing it has going for it is that it stops bullets.

Insignia as Target?

One veteran superhero explained, in an award-winning memoir, that he had chosen to wear a bright insignia on the chest of his otherwise dark costume because he could not armor his mask. His idea, then, was to draw enemy fire toward his torso. Precise enemy fire, presumably. If you are likewise of the mind that it is better to be shot where it is convenient for you, then consider wearing your high-contrast insignia where you would least mind being wounded. Your shoulder, perhaps. Or your car.

Insignia

It is vital that your insignia be closely and clearly related to your superhero identity. Nothing interferes with the swift execution of justice like having to interrupt a fight to explain to a villain who, exactly, you are.

Your insignia must also strike fear into the hearts of evildoers. Criminals are a cowardly, superstitious lot, and insignias relating to destiny can be remarkably effective. You might want to indicate the bad luck you intend to visit upon wrongdoers—for example, by displaying the number 13, or a broken mirror, or an image of character actor William H.

Macy, who is well known for his many portrayals of luckless losers. Or you might want your insignia to suggest the good fortune that shines upon you in battle—for example, with a four-leaf clover, or a horseshoe, or an image of character actor William H. Macy, who is lucky enough to land interesting and challenging roles.

Yes

No

Once again, don't be ashamed to seek help. If you are a reclusive multimillionaire, you can simply hire a top-quality graphic designer. Otherwise, look for world-famous artists who have been trapped inside the twisted worlds of their own paintings by uncanny mystical forces. If you release them from eerie nightmare realms of their own making, they are likely to offer their services for free.

Another Table

Superhero Name	Good Insignia	Bad Insignia
THE EAGLE	A bald eagle in flight	Mr. Clean in a hang-glider
HOTSPUR	The dogs of war	The dogs of war playing poker
CAPTAIN VENGEANCE	A bloody skull	Mahatma Gandhi
THE FLAMING SWORD	A flaming sword	Something that is neither swordlike nor aflame

The Strange Case of
MR. MANDELBROT,
THE CHAOS CRUSADER

Your insignia must be simple enough that even the youngest sidekick can draw it in the dust with his foot moments before he is kidnapped by your archenemy; that way, the police who arrive on the scene moments too late will know whom to contact. Learn from the sad example of MR. MANDELBROT, THE CHAOS CRUSADER. In 1987, his loyal

Teen sidekick DOT shown here summoning THE TELEGRAPH

assistant, THE EFFECTIVE BUTTERFLY, was kidnapped by their archenemy, THE ENGLISH MAJOR. For some fifteen years, THE EFFECTIVE BUTTERFLY held his hands in front of a candle while trying to form his fingers into the shape of MR. MANDELBROT's logo, so that MR. MANDELBROT, seeing his symbol silhouetted against the wall of the nearby office building where he worked, would come to the rescue of his faithful friend.

Alas, because MR. MANDELBROT's logo was a theoretical shape of mathematically infinite complexity, this proved difficult. Ultimately, THE ENGLISH MAJOR was arrested on unrelated charges of selling hard cider without a license, and THE EFFECTIVE BUTTERFLY was freed, but the experience left the unfortunate sidekick with a crippling case of arthritis.

Costume Construction (and Repair)

If you have planned ahead, you will have been raised by an elderly relative whose failing eyesight belies her remarkable facility for knitting, enabling her to construct the most elaborate of costumes without realizing your secret identity.

If not, *you* must learn how to sew. In the long run, this skill will not be wasted. After fighting the most powerful enemies in one-on-one battles that leave entire city blocks pulverized, your costume might get torn. Indeed, in the most extreme circumstances, your cape might become tattered, causing it to flap dramatically behind you as you stand backlit by the sunset atop what was once a building, now pulverized.

Changing into Your Costume

Even the best costume is of little use if you are unable to change into it discreetly. You will have to decide whether to wear your costume under your clothes at all times, or carry it with you and change when the need arises.

As with so many decisions regarding your newly chosen profession, there is no clear right or wrong in this matter, and you must weigh the pros and cons for yourself. On one hand, wearing your costume under your civilian clothes might cause awkward moments when disrobing in front of your one true love, who remains unaware of your secret identity. On the other hand, this impediment to your love life might also prevent you from falling for a beautiful woman who turns out to be your shape-shifting archenemy, MR. MIRAGE.

MR. MIRAGE, master of disguise.

CHAPTER THREE

EQUIPPING YOURSELF FOR SUPERHEROICS

Your name, when mentioned, will suggest moral rectitude. Your symbol, when projected onto a clear night sky, or incorporated as a watermark or in the letterhead of your stationery, will represent good judgment. Your costume, when you wear it to the scene of a crime, will assure others that the evildoers will be apprehended, perhaps by you. But then, when the time comes to act, when your mostly intangible *accoutrements* have served their respective purposes, will you proceed armed with your brawn and/or brains alone? Or will you be aided in your crusading by devices and doohickeys—equipment, in a word? If the latter, then just what equipment, exactly? And where, pray tell, on your running, leaping, swinging, swooping, costume-clad person will you carry this extra poundage and ounceage?

Not Every Superhero Runs

Maybe you do not plan to do much running, or jogging even. You might be the lumbering type of superhero. If that is the case, and if you foresee needing to haul heavy equipment in keeping with your persona, then you should feel free to do just that. If you are going to be GARBAGE-MAN, and in the early morning hours you will pick up the refuse of society, arresting human detritus in oversize plastic barrels . . . well, that much more power to you.

The Basics

To begin, find or make room for the following:

Money. Money will allow you to purchase other supplies and sometimes cooperation, as necessary and appropriate.

Keys. If you drive or pilot a supervehicle of any kind, you of course will want to keep with you at all times the means of opening it and starting it up.

Watch. Ideally, your watch will switch between civilian time (*4:18 A.M., 12 noon*) and superhero time (*clobbering time, half past clobbering time*).

Where to Stick It

Time was, whatever you carried had to fit on your belt or in your boot. Since then, though, superheroes have gotten quite creative. One, a cape-wearer, was inspired to sew a pouch into his cape, to secret there his eyeglasses, some say. Others report it was his date book.

The trend away from tights toward less constrictive and revealing costume materials is accompanied by greater opportunities for incorporating compartments in one's vestments. THE SCHOOLGIRL, for example, though perhaps principally clad in a skirt-and-sweater ensemble, might carry a knapsack. Become BAG-LADY, and push a shopping cart. THE LUGGER could—nay, *should*—tote luggage.

Survival of the Outfittest

Experts agree that mere survival depends on your having also these ten items:

1. *Map.* An up-to-date combination bus/subway map and schedule is best;

2. *Flashlight.* A battery-operated flashlight is useful for illuminating dark places such as alleys, ventilation ducts, elevator shafts, stairwells, and candlelit villains' lairs;

3. *Food.* Food is good to eat if you get hungry;

4. *Water.* Water is good for washing off blood, yours or otherwise;

5. *Knife.* A knife is useful for cutting things;

6. *Rope.* Rope is useful for tying things together;

7. *Matches.* Or a lighter, in case the batteries in your flashlight die;

8. *Mirror.* For checking your face for cuts and scratches;

9. *First-aid kit.* To offer the other guy after a fight; and

10. *Sunglasses.* In a pinch, sunglasses can substitute for your civilian clothing, should you need to disguise your superhero persona; contrariwise, they can substitute for your superhero costume, should you need to disguise your civilian identity.

Local Notions

All the world is perhaps a stage, but you will probably be staging at least the majority of your superheroics in three spheres: the urban, the suburban, and the rural realms.

For city work, you will want to carry a substantial amount of change; public telephones are expensive and are ever becoming more so. Also make sure you have an umbrella, as it tends to rain suddenly and severely in the city. Have pepper spray (for use on rodents and rodentlike birds). Aspirin is essential, as are earplugs.

In the suburbs, carry a library card, an automatic teller machine card, and a supermarket discount card. Have pepper spray (for use on stray, menacing dogs). Pack a bottle opener.

Rural duty calls for an atlas, bread crumbs, a pup tent, sunscreen, pepper spray (for use on feral, possibly rabid deer, on local residents, and on the nefarious villain THE FERAL, POSSIBLY RABID DEER), and antidepressants.

Specialized Equipment

What other equipment you carry depends in part on your persona, and the more specific your persona, the more specialized your equipment.

If you are the stealthy sort, given to picking locks, cracking safes, and neatly short-circuiting state-of-the-art security systems, you will carry: a lockpick and a safecrack, as well as a length of wire, a hairnet, and a balloon, though it would be irresponsible of the authors to spell out here how, exactly, to employ these items.

On the other hand, if you are the obvious type, you might equip yourself with a sword, a shield, a horse, and *several* balloons.

THE BATTING COACH might tote a Louisville Slugger. SCARLET SECRETARY should have a notepad with her at all times.

Signature Equipment

It should go without saying that if your equipment, or some item of it, is so intimately connected with your superhero persona that you have named yourself for the

Top to Bottom: The Studebaker of Solitude, the Plymouth of Power, the Rolls Royce of Righteousness, and the Duesenberg of Domestic Tranquility

item, then you must have it with you always. If you are THE BEACHBALL because you are as wide as you are tall and your costume is made of brightly colored strips of plastic, fine. But if you are THE BEACHBALL because your primary, perhaps only, tool of the trade is a beachball (of justice, rightfulness, what have you), then you had better have that beachball on or near your person. And an air pump, to be safe. (In the alternative, consider taking on a sidekick, PUMP-BOY, who naturally must follow this same rule. If you do carry the Beachball of Justice, though, then PUMP-BOY should carry a foot pump of *triumph*, perhaps, and not the hand pump of justice. A Beachball of Justice *inflated with justice* would be a bit much.)

New and/or Improved Equipment

Besides the equipment that you buy from a store (convenience, department, religious supply, or otherwise) and the mystical equipment that slips into your downstairs linen closet from another dimension, there is a third kind of equipment—specifically, stuff you know you want but that is not commercially or interdimensionally available and that you, therefore, must make yourself. Of this kind of equipment, there are two varieties: extraordinary stuff, and ordinary stuff that you would prefer to re-create in your image. Let us consider the second of these first.

Envision yourself THE GIZMOMANOMETER, and your persona so heavily dependent upon the availability of the "right tools" for the job that your costume is fairly overflowing with gear. It would not do for you to get around on a mundane motorcycle: You must ride a Gizmotorcycle. You will eavesdrop on your prey with a Gizmonitor. To help you see, from time to time, you will raise your Gizmonocle. And when hurt you will inject Gizmorphine into your Gizmoneymaker.

On the other hand, if your brand of superheroism requires the employment of a projectile weapon that fires disloyal employees, for example, or some sort of hypnotic Magic Marker, you had best get inventing.

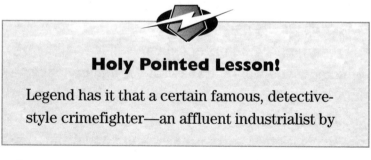

Holy Pointed Lesson!

Legend has it that a certain famous, detective-style crimefighter—an affluent industrialist by day—had invested years and millions in developing a pen specifically for use in his night crusading. The prototype, when finished, wrote upside down, underwater, and on almost any surface (including glass), and functioned even at extreme temperatures.

One night, on a stakeout with his sidekick, a young contortionist he had recently acquired from a traveling Petrogradian circus, our superhero reached into his belt for his custom-made pen, intending to make note of something he had just observed or overheard, when he noticed the boy produce a writing implement of his own.

"What's that, chum?" the superhero asked.

"A pencil," replied the sidekick. "It works anywhere, under any condition."

The superhero reached over, took hold of the lad's pencil, and with his gauntleted hand snapped off the point.

"How about now?" the superhero asked.

Keep Your Equipment Clean (and Loaded)

To ensure the safe and dependable operation of your equipment, you must keep your equipment clean and (if necessary) properly lubricated. Make it your regular practice to clean your equipment when you return home from fighting crime; do not expect to have time to do it when duty next calls. It is especially important that you clean your equipment whenever it has been exposed to rain, dirt, mud, snow, sleet, saltwater, or electromagnetic interference. Keep your less-often-used equipment free of rust and dust. Keep all of your equipment free of debris and alien microorganisms.

(On a related note: Disengage any removable power sources before storing equipment.)

As important as keeping your equipment serviceable, though, *is keeping it loaded*, if it is that kind of equipment. If your helmet-mounted paralysis-froth cannon requires froth-fluid, SPITFIRE, for the love of all things good, keep the tank full! Do not find yourself in the midst of a chase, WEED WARRIOR, with triggers pumping, but with no Jimson discs in your Jimson-jingal!

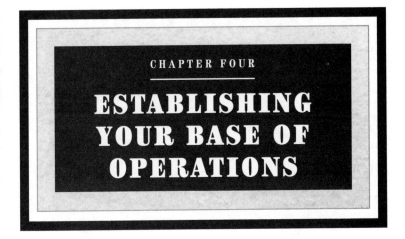

CHAPTER FOUR

ESTABLISHING YOUR BASE OF OPERATIONS

You do not have any control over where you will fight crime. Your battles will take place wherever evil might lurk: amongst the shifting shadows of vampire-filled forests, or in the accounting departments of major corporations. But where you retire after battle—to heal your wounds, plan your next move, and turn dials on large computer panels full of flashing lights—is very much up to you.

THE REAL-ESTATE AGENT'S Rallying Cry

"Look, honey, our first secret headquarters. And there's extra room if we want to have sidekicks some day."

In establishing your secret base, remember the rallying cry of the fearless REAL-ESTATE AGENT: "Location, location, location—and away!"

That does not mean, though, that every superhero will consider the same location to be ideal. Certainly, one will find the highest concentration of heroes in big cities like Centralopolis or Metrotopia. But the possibilities are limitless. One might prefer to perch an aerie high atop the Eiffel Tower, while another might prefer to tuck his lair inside the dark recesses of a subway station, or to miniaturize it and fit it into the tiniest microcorner of a single atom. A further option is to rent office space in one of the many economically depressed cities, such as Buffalo, New York, which currently offer substantial tax incentives to relocating superheroes.

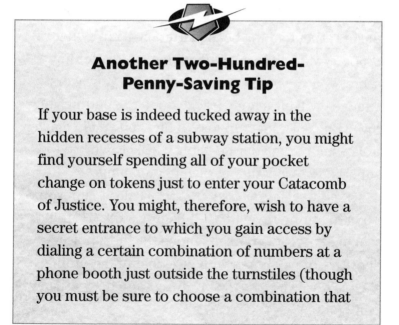

Another Two-Hundred-Penny-Saving Tip

If your base is indeed tucked away in the hidden recesses of a subway station, you might find yourself spending all of your pocket change on tokens just to enter your Catacomb of Justice. You might, therefore, wish to have a secret entrance to which you gain access by dialing a certain combination of numbers at a phone booth just outside the turnstiles (though you must be sure to choose a combination that is toll-free). If this proves impractical, consider purchasing a monthly fare-saver pass.

Protecting Property Values

As a super-paragon of community service, you will no doubt wish to consider the impact that a new, state-of-the-art crimefighting headquarters will have on local property values. Keep in mind that, no matter how secret you wish your secret base to be, your worst enemies will ultimately track you there, putting your loved ones in danger of loss of life, and you in danger of lawsuits from your neighbors. This is why so few superheroes operate out of condominiums.

Of course, if you are CAPTAIN LIBRARIAN, and you do battle primarily with the villainous ENEMY MIME, you might locate yourself among the most noise-sensitive of neighbors with little fear of disturbing them. Otherwise, try to stay away from busy urban centers.

If You Must Live in a City

"Welcome to Buffalo."

Sometimes, a crowded metropolitan area is your only option, for financial, logistical, or elderly-aunt-tending reasons. If this is the case, remember that many districts require extensive site impact reports before any new superhero construction, in order to mitigate concerns regarding noise, giant alien death rays, and additional traffic. The exceptions, once again, are economically depressed cities like Buffalo, New York, which tend to view the massive destruction wrought by alien death rays as an integral part of the urban renewal process.

A Superhero's Giant Flaming Sword of Justice Is His or Her Castle

Before construction can begin on your secret superhero hideaway, you must choose a theme for it. Will it be a hall? A fortress? A gigantic rotating representation of a common household object?

Once you have chosen a shape, you will need to add to it an appellation. Anybody with sufficient disposable income can live in a tower; only a superhero can live in a Tower of Justice.

One issue that need not concern you is keeping your hideout inconspicuous. Thanks to modern holographic technology, heroes and villains routinely construct massive, five hundred–story edifices in the most obvious of public places, and local civilians are none the wiser. For example, the next time you see a photograph of the Lincoln Memorial, examine it carefully. No matter how closely you look, you will not see, looming overhead, the thousand-foot-tall Log

Cabin of Justice wherein THE GREAT EMANCIPATOR ponders his next move in the never-ending battle against the villainous REBEL YELL.

So let your imagination run wild. As the table below sets out, the possibilities are limitless.

Good Hideaways

- The Fortress of Justice
- The Hall of Solitude
- The Laboratory of Justice
- The Giant Flying Dragon of Solitary Justice
- The Justly Solitary Fortress-Hall of Solicitous Justitude

Bad Hideaways

- The Frat House of Keggers
- The Hair and Nail Salon of Mild Disapproval
- The Mosh Pit of Unregulated Electronic File-Swapping
- The Run-Down Old Burger Joint of Reasonably Good Behavior
- Joe's House of Stuff

Owning Versus Renting

Ideally, you will own your own base of operations, allowing you to build up equity for your retirement. The crusader who does not put something aside might find himself in the unenviable position of the once-estimable INEVITABLE INVINCIBLE, whose late-night infomercials for adult waterproof undergarments were an embarrassment to superheroes everywhere.

Legal Precautions

First, make sure that any property you purchase or rent is either exclusively in the name of your superhero persona or exclusively in the name of your civilian identity. Deeds and rental agreements are public documents, and local property records offices are typically the first stops of crusading reporters who wish to uncover the mysterious secrets of glamorous superheroes.

If you are renting property, pay particularly close attention to the tenant application form. A common technique of supervillains is to purchase residential rental property in neighborhoods with high superhero concentrations in the hope of stumbling upon the civilian identities of their crimefighting foes/tenants. Here is an example of an actual application form seized by the City of Buffalo's ever-vigilant Department of Landlord-Supertenant Relations. Can you spot the warning signs?

MAIN STREET
APARTMENTS OF JUSTICE

TENANT APPLICATION FORM

CIVILIAN NAME: _____

SUPERHERO NAME: _____

PLEASE PROVIDE THREE REFERENCES
(Note: At least one must be from your current employer,
and at least one must be a personal reference from a
youthful sidekick whom you rescued from a local
orphanage.)

_____

_____

_____

EMERGENCY CONTACT: _____

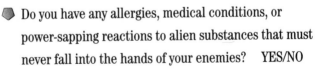

- Do you have any allergies, medical conditions, or
power-sapping reactions to alien substances that must
never fall into the hands of your enemies?   YES/NO

- Do you smoke?   YES/NO

Fortifying Your Fortress

Intend it though you might to be a place of relaxation, introspection, and epiphany-having, your base of operations will prove an irresistible target to the ne'er-do-wells you are sworn to combat. It is, therefore, vital that you build into it adequate security. A radar on the roof, six-inch-thick titanium shielding on exterior walls, and giant-glass-plates-that-drop-down-over-interior-doorways-while-rooms-fill-up-with-sleeping-gas are musts.

Once you have taken care of the basics, you might wish to tailor additional security to your own personal needs. If, for example, you have meddled once too often in the world-conquering plans of VICTOR VICTORIAN, you might need additional protection against armies of tightly corseted nannybots pushing explosive perambulators.

Beauty Is Truth, Truth Beauty

A properly armored Lair of Justice need not be unattractive—far from it. As EL MODERNISTE's famous Frank Gehry–designed Museum of Solitude in Bilbao, Spain, proves, titanium shielding can be a thing of considerable grace. Even those without EL MODERNISTE's extensive budget can use their creativity to make beauty out of necessity. If you need inspiration, THE INTERIOR DECORATOR's remarkable Bleecker Street Hall of Fabulosity is open to the public when its owner is not busy fighting MR. LAST YEAR.

Better, Faster, Stronger

The time you spend in your base will not be purely recreational. If you wish to remain at the top of your game, you will need to constantly train, and a properly equipped lair can help you do so.

You will, of course, wish to invest in: a basic assortment of free weights for strength training; a treadmill for speed training; a rowing machine for capturing-evil-coxswain training; a climbing wall for rescuing-innocent-victims-left-in-vultures'-nests training; and a washing machine to clean your towels.

If your lair is hidden somewhere in your civilian home, you will also want to invest in a good ventilation system. Nothing gives away your secret identity faster than the distinctive smell of superhero sweat wafting through an ordinary-seeming house.

Not to Mention Smarter

A wise hero will not neglect the need for mental training, as well. A chessboard will help keep your wits sharp; a chess-playing robot companion will sharpen them further; and if that robot companion has an endearingly human sense of humor, you might sharpen your wit as well as your wits.

No matter how clever you might be, though, you will occasionally need help deciphering mysterious clues, or translating messages from aliens. For tasks that are only slightly beyond the human intellect, you might depend on your robot chess opponent. Particularly difficult challenges, however, might cause his positronic brain to explode in a dangerous shower of sparks. For tough conundrums, therefore, you will want to purchase a supercomputer or, in certain extreme circumstances, a mega-computer.

Choosing a computer is simple. You merely need to purchase the largest one with the most flashing lights that your budget will allow.

CHAPTER FIVE

MAINTAINING (AND REVEALING) YOUR SECRET IDENTITY

Reportedly, it has been said that it is easier to tell the truth than to lie, and by analogy to come forth than to keep a secret. A hero, however, has little choice—unless she has no family, no friends, and no pets whose consciences would be shocked or whose safety would be compromised by the truth. Your new persona, your superhero identity, is a secret, and it must be ever thus, else your enemies might threaten what is important to Civilian You to gain the upper hand against Superhero You.

Still and all, the necessity of secrecy is often tempered by the desire to confide in one or more persons to keep from going crazy. If you are to share your secret, you had best think long and hard about whom you will tell. Although unburdening yourself will likely bring great relief, you will have to consider the effect that your revelation will have on your parents, your significant other, or the other students in your creative writing workshop.

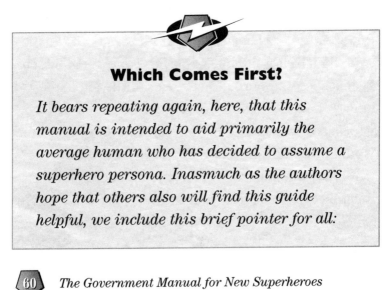

Which Comes First?

It bears repeating again, here, that this manual is intended to aid primarily the average human who has decided to assume a superhero persona. Inasmuch as the authors hope that others also will find this guide helpful, we include this brief pointer for all:

It is not always obvious which persona is one's first. Consider that there are some superheroes—aliens and mutants, mainly—for whom the regular human persona is the one later adopted. For the regular human, it is the other way around.

As a practical matter, it does not matter which persona comes first: *When you are employing one persona, you must keep the other secret.*

How to Keep a Secret

Perhaps the most effective way to keep your secret is to forget it yourself, but then you could hardly be expected to remember that you are a superhero when it is time for you to be superheroic. There is no way that you would also remember the *details* of your superhero persona, such as whether your cape goes on colored-side out, or which belt compartment holds your closed-circuit heliox rebreather, or where you parked your Super-Segway. (Hypnotism, with all due respect to THE MESMERER, is not reliable.)

So you will have to keep your other identity secret while still keeping it in mind. Keeping a secret under this circumstance, then, is mainly just a matter of *not doing* certain things:

- When in civilian mode, do not tell others that you are a superhero. Conversely, when you are in superhero mode, do not let on who you are the rest of the time with any specificity, even if you must forgo an opportunity to advance your civilian career or that of a close friend or relative. For example, if your father is a glazier, you must keep yourself from handing out his business card even after a battle that leaves many large storefront windows shattered.
- Do not carry your superhero identification card in your civilian wallet, and vice versa.
- Do not acknowledge your dual identity in writing. Do not endorse personal or business correspondence, "Jeff Jarndyce a/k/a FLAPJACK."

- Do not open a bank account with both your civilian persona and your superhero persona as signatories, as in, "Marla Moppe and THE EXECUTRIX, *as joint owners with right of survivorship.*" In a similar vein, your superhero persona should not guaranty loans made to your civilian persona.

On the other hand, there are certain things that you might have to do, affirmatively, from time to time, to maintain your facade, including:

- Muffle your voice, perhaps with your civilian sleeve, when speaking on a telephone, if you are supposed to be conversing or leaving a message in your superhero persona but you are in fact in your civilian persona and garb. Note: This is necessary only if, as a superhero, you wear a mask that muffles your voice.
- If you have been invited, as a superhero, to a formal event, wear a tuxedo or gown *over* your full costume.

Declining Credit

Keeping your superhero identity secret means not being too obviously or exclusively supportive of your superhero persona. Worse, it means often not being able to bask in the adoration and adulation of the public when you are out of costume. Worst of all, on occasion, you might actually have to join in bouts of public verbal bashing of your superhero alter ego. Example:

Your boss (unwittingly): That FINE SAMARITAN is a menace!

You (unwillingly): Yeah.

The Coincidence Conundrum

Imagine having to hear this, from a coworker or good friend: "J. Joshua Johnson, whenever trouble arises you are never anywhere to be found! Come to think of it, you, J. Joshua Johnson, disappear when the astonishing, wonderful, and likely fertile PEREGRINE shows up. . . ."

Sooner or later, someone is going to observe and remark that you in fact do disappear whenever trouble arises, and that you are indeed never around when your superhero persona is. This observant and talkative person, if he or she is also good at math, is going to put the proverbial two and two together and conclude that you and your superhero persona are one. That will be an awkward moment for both of you—or all three of you.

Dealing with the Secret Sharer

If this unintended sharer of your secret, this nosy, intrusive busybody, is habitually indiscreet, your options are few: silence him or her forever, or take him or her under your wing, officially, as your sidekick. If contemplating the first of these options does not immediately fill you with horror and revulsion, please put down this book immediately, as you are clearly a supervillain (although not, we trust, so villainous as to continue reading this book after being politely asked not to do so). All other readers are invited to turn to Chapter Six for the details of making someone your sidekick.

Whom to Tell

Maybe nothing escapes the notice of your manservant—not the draft in the Porcelain Table Room, not the water ring on the Pembroke, not that you go out every night and often by way of a fourth-floor window. Maybe the other reporter with whom your common editor has teamed you was born at night, but it was not last night, and besides, you are in love with her. Maybe you want Mom and Dad to trust you again now that you are in your early twenties. Your valet, your colleague, your parents: These, then, are the persons you will consider letting in on your secret, provided you are sure that they can keep your secret themselves. On the other hand, though, what of your ancient aunt, whose longevity is rivaled only by the depth of her dislike for your superhero persona? Your revelation might be the death of her!

It would be presumptuous and time-consuming, among other things, for the authors of this modest guide to make recommendations regarding whom to tell about your secret identity. You cannot expect to substitute institutional wisdom for your own judgment. However, this manual can address how you might break the news to a new confidant(e).

Breaking the News

There is a long-forgotten fable about the man who travels out of town, leaving his beloved cat in the care of his brother. When the man first calls home from the road to inquire about his cat's well-being, his brother informs him that the cat is dead. The man is horrified, both by the news and by the delivery, and he chastises his brother, suggesting that a better way to deal the blow would have been to build up to it over several phone calls. The first time he called, the man explains, his brother could have reported that the man's cat had run away. The second time, that the cat was on the roof. Next, that the cat had slipped and fallen and was in the pet hospital. And so on. The brother takes the advice to heart, and when the man calls next and inquires about the health of their mother, the brother reports, "She's *my* mother. You were adopted."

"That's right, Billy. Dead."

Like the brother in the fable, you will do better not to drop a bomb into anyone's lap, as it were. You will want to introduce the idea of your being superheroic gradually, so as not to disturb anyone overmuch. Rather than announce, "I'm the ORNATE GADROON!" you might say, "I see you've gotten your hair cut. Have you ever noticed that in the summer months I tend to tan more on my cheeks than around my eyes, where a small mask might go . . . ?"

Expect Some Resistance

Unfortunately, you cannot assume that, because you have chosen to tell someone that you are a superhero, that person will be glad to know as much. For some, it is an uninvited burden, having to keep your secret, and the person who feels that way really cannot be faulted. If she wanted to keep such a secret, perhaps she would have become a superhero herself.

There are others, though, who will think it unnatural, unhealthy even, that you are superheroic. They will suggest that being a superhero is a choice, nothing more, and that you can choose *not* to be a superhero. These persons, too, are correct: It *is* unnatural to be a superhero, else you would have been born with superpowers; it *is* unhealthy— exercising daily in a gym, where there are no supervillains, would be much healthier; and it *is* your choice. You were not forced into it—other than by your abiding love of freedom and justice.

The Upside of Revelation

More likely than not, though, if you reveal your duality to a good friend, lover, or relative, that person will be appreciative of the difficulty of your decision, flattered by your trust, and impressed by your courage, and he or she will ask you to get autographs of certain other superheroes, assuming that each superhero knows every other superhero. Your confidant(e) will feel closer to you than ever before. You will probably not regret the revelation of your secret identity, and, besides, getting it off your chest will leave that much more room for your awe-inspiring insignia.

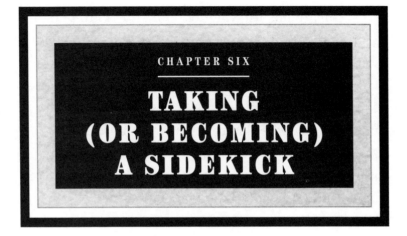

CHAPTER SIX

TAKING (OR BECOMING) A SIDEKICK

A Sidekick Is Not for Every Superhero

Before you made the decision to don cape, cowl, belt, and boots, did you dream of being a superhero? In your fantasies, did you work alone, or were you accompanied in your crusading by another—perhaps someone who ran, flew, swam, or posed just behind you? Not every superhero needs a sidekick, and not every superhero would be comfortable having one.

If you are unsure whether your superhero persona contraindicates your taking on a sidekick, you might consider your name and nothing else. If you have adopted a name like THE SOUND, BEDKNOBS, or DARRYL HALL, then you should find your lesser half with all haste. On the other hand, if you are SOLE-MAN, THE LONE RACCOON, or AUTONOMOUS SOVEREIGN, you probably did not expect ever to work with others, and you are encouraged to stay the course.

With Great Authority Comes Great Accountability

The role of a superhero principal is that of *mentor* to a sidekick. Experts agree that an inspiring, effective mentor is one who, among other things: has respect for and trusts the learner; can provide a framework for exploration by creating a context that provides support and encouragement; and will not allow unsupervised parties in the hideout or hand over the keys to the supervehicle without getting the sidekick's promise to return at a reasonable hour, having refilled the fuel tanks or recharged the power cells.

Screening and Selecting a Sidekick

If you are in the market for a sidekick, you might start from scratch—posting notices and placing ads in trade papers and on bulletin boards at the grocery store, soliciting and reviewing confidential applications, setting up interviews, calling back the strong candidates, sending out rejection letters. Or you might offer the position to someone you already know, and presumably trust, and who maybe has already impressed you by figuring out your secret identity.

Regardless how you find your sidekick, you will be looking for certain qualities in the ward whom you will trust to keep your confidences and to help you out of your costume. First among them is trustworthiness. Then good balance. You will want by your side someone who unbosoms freely, advises justly, assists readily, adventures boldly, takes all patiently, defends courageously, and continues unchangeably.

Also, your sidekick must not be better than you are at anything.

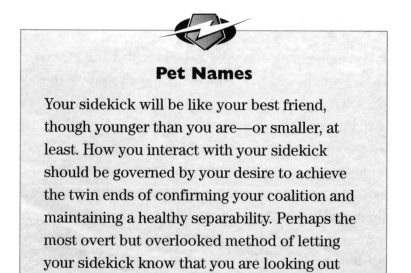

Pet Names

Your sidekick will be like your best friend, though younger than you are—or smaller, at least. How you interact with your sidekick should be governed by your desire to achieve the twin ends of confirming your coalition and maintaining a healthy separability. Perhaps the most overt but overlooked method of letting your sidekick know that you are looking out for him or her, though from a distance, is by addressing your assistant appropriately.

You will want to address your sidekick as "kid" often, and likewise refer to him or her as "the kid." You might also try addressing your sidekick as "lad/lass," "pal," or "buddy." Use the term "partner" sparingly, and only if you are sure it will not give your sidekick the wrong idea regarding the equality of your contributions to the fight against crime and evil. "Junior," on the other hand, is perfectly appropriate. Also, "Plan B."

Leaving the Kid at Home

You might find yourself one day or night wanting to go it alone, to fly solo, to capture red-handed baddies single-handedly—that is, without your sidekick in tow. You want some time just for you and your archenemy.

You might find yourself feeling guilty for having this desire. Do not. You have chosen for a protégé someone mature, if rough around the edges, and whether it is for your sidekick's own safety that you want him or her to stay back and dust the megacomputer, or for your own sanity, you have the final say, and the good sidekick will understand and obey. The *excellent* sidekick, by contrast, will disobey, arriving at the lair of your archenemy just in time to save you from otherwise certain death.

Starting Out as a Sidekick

Maybe you wonder if your thoughts are normal, wanting as you do to be a sidekick yourself, doubtful as you are that you are ready to be your own super man or woman, preferring as you would to test the waters of superheroism with your booted big toe. After all, why would anyone want to be a sidekick? A side *dish* is never as fashionable as the main course. . . .

Or is it? Some restaurants, trading on the popularity of their side dishes, now offer a "meal of sides"—that is, a combination platter composed of only side dishes, three or four of them, *with no main dish.* Consider the Spanish *tapas*, the French *amuse bouche*, the Turkish *mezze*, and the Cantonese *dim sum.*

We will therefore address the remainder of this chapter to the *tapas* of the superhero world. (We are speaking in purely metaphorical terms, of course. The reader who is interested in the literal *tapas* of the superhero world is advised to seek out the seminal work on the subject, *Las Tapas Del Mundo De Las Personas Que Luchan Contra El Crimen*, by famed superchef EL BULI.)

The Apprentice System

Time was, one who desired to learn a craft or trade, intending to make such craft or trade his life's work, became apprenticed to a master crafts—or tradesman. An apprentice helped his master in every way imaginable; in return, the master imparted unto his apprentice invaluable knowledge, wisdom, and insight. Substituting *sidekick* for "apprentice," *superhero* for "master," and *detective techniques, small arms practice,* and *martial arts training* for "knowledge, wisdom, and insight" should give you an idea of how little has changed in seven hundred years.

Special Considerations

Your principal most likely wants your sidekick persona to complement his or her superhero persona, though some prefer an opposite associate.

Consider, for example, such master-servant arrangements as: LAMPLIGHTER and helper BOY BUTANE; THE BRIDE and her two subordinates, BRIDESMAID and GROOM; and GIN and TONIC.

On the other hand, MORAY-MAN lets SUNFISH tag along. Likewise, THE WHIG is training TORY TOT.

Before you commit to anything—before you make a nonrefundable deposit on a costume or order a vanity license plate—you must discuss the matter with your superhero and reach an understanding.

The Responsibilities of a Sidekick

You will be your superhero's right-hand man, or man-child, or "man Friday," albeit every day of the week, and often at night. Your principal will expect your unwavering loyalty, your undivided attention, and your help getting home from the semiannual Super Semi-Formal at the Dance Hall of Justice.

You will have to take the wheel, stick, or reins of the supervehicle to enable your principal to leap from it onto another vehicle of comparable speed.

You will have to hand over your weapon to your principal so that he might take the shot, even if you have a better line of sight.

And you will have to fish equipment from your principal's belt, boot, or pocket when you two are tied together, back to back.

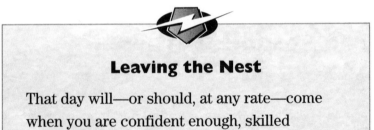

Leaving the Nest

That day will—or should, at any rate—come when you are confident enough, skilled enough, and well-enough trained to be your own superhero. Or you are just too old to be a sidekick any longer. Go back to Chapter One.

No One Succeeds Like a Sidekick

As sidekick to your superhero, you are like a firstborn child, at least inasmuch as it is your prerogative to succeed to the persona of your principal, if you so choose, upon his or her temporary indisposition, permanent retirement, or unreported death. Your principal will not bestow this honor to another unless intentionally to slight you, perhaps after an irretrievable breakdown of your working relationship that is the culmination of years of largely unaddressed hostility between you that has only increased as you have gotten older while he or she has seemed not to age.

But, assuming that things remain both hunky and dory between you, by the time your principal is ready to place the mantle on the mantle, so to speak, you will have been groomed to take over the job, and you will slip into the role as smoothly as you will slip into the garb, provided that your principal did not have the costume taken out as he or she put on weight in the later years, as THE KING did. The transition will be seamless and the world will be none the wiser (unless you need to update the superhero persona to fit the times, as did the incoming BUFFALO NICKEL, THE MULLET, and BETA MAX).

CHAPTER SEVEN

TEAMING UP

Bad guys, by definition, do not play fair. You can no doubt defeat the dastardly DARK DEMON on his own, but he will have no compunction about joining forces with the devilish DASTARD DREADNOUGHT and the demonic DEVIL DAME in an effort to overwhelm you with sheer force of both numbers and alliteration. Faced with such unsportsmanlike behavior, you will wish to make the odds more even by enlisting allies of your own. Although you already have truth, justice, and the American way on your side, there will be occasions when you will be grateful for the assistance of the unbelievable TRUTH, the military JUSTICE, and the American WAY as well.

Super-Allies Wanted

Finding a team to join can be trickier than you might imagine. There is, after all, a reason why most organizations use the word "secret" in describing their headquarters. Even if you should succeed in locating one, marching up to the front door and knocking is likely to elicit only the polite insistence that this gleaming marble skyscraper is simply the location of Joe's Plumbing Supplies, just like the sign says.

Fortunately, you might find yourself acquiring allies naturally in the course of your normal crime-fighting routine. For example, if you are attempting to track down THE KILLER CREAM PUFF, you might discover countless clues pointing you toward the trendy-but-menacing Restaurant of Death on 43rd and Presidential, over by the Centralville City Hall. Disguising yourself as a short-order fry cook, you might then obtain employment and soon find your suspicions piqued by a weaselly looking busboy who always seems to disappear moments before THE KILLER CREAM PUFF makes an entrance. Shadowing him one

"Secret headquarters? What secret headquarters?"

rain-soaked night, you might momentarily lose sight of
him, only to have him leap on you from around the
corner of a deserted alleyway. After an epic battle, you
would most likely discover that he is actually the
noble MARSHAL MELLOW, and that he had been led to the
Restaurant of Death by the very same trail of clues
that brought you there. After bandaging your wounds,
the two of you would then reluctantly enter into a
grudging joint pursuit of THE KILLER CREAM PUFF,
gradually discovering that your initial uneasy truce

has blossomed into a full-fledged friendship, and from there into an indissoluble partnership.

You might also try looking in the classifieds under "Super-Allies Wanted."

Avoiding Embarrassment

There is no greater source of chagrin for the costume-wearing righteous than inadvertently joining a team of supervillains. Here are some warning signs that your newfound teammates are actually on the opposing side.

- Their headquarters is called "The _____ of Doom" rather than "The _____ of Justice."

- Their computers are tended by indistinguishable, frequently incompetent technicians in white lab coats.

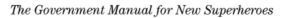

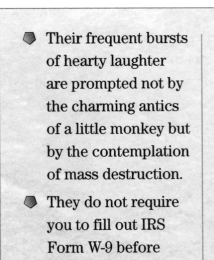

- Their frequent bursts of hearty laughter are prompted not by the charming antics of a little monkey but by the contemplation of mass destruction.

- They do not require you to fill out IRS Form W-9 before joining them.

If this man is just pouring liquids back and forth, then he works for an evil organization. Steer clear!

Finding a Good Fit

Do not let your need for allies push you into joining a team where you do not belong. If you have become a master of the martial arts after years of studying in a remote Shaolin monastery, will you really be comfortable in the glitzy Manhattan hideout of the SOCIALITES OF LIBERTY? On the other hand, if your secret identity as a millionaire dandy has made sipping cocktails with the wealthy elite seem tedious, the sparse wooden shack of the APPALACHIAN AVENGERS might be exactly what you need.

The Sad Story of the *Birds of a Feather*

In civilian life, individuals of similar interests and abilities often enjoy congregating together. But alas! A principle that might be well-suited to dinner parties is disastrous when applied to superhero teams. The outlooks of your cohorts should be akin, but their abilities must not be identical. Take note of the unhappy experience of the BIRDS OF A FEATHER, whose members included THE SPARROW, THE WREN, LADY HAWK, and THE JOLLY ROBIN. Mighty champions though they were, the entire team was wiped out moments into its very first excursion by the menacing JET ENGINE.

Dealing with Rejection

Do not be hurt if your application to join a team is turned down. A supersociety might have an opening for a hero with very specific abilities, and the members' decision that you do not fit their current needs is not a personal slight. Applicants who respond to rejection by becoming evil and devoting themselves to the destruction of the offending heroes are rarely invited to apply for future openings, no matter how remorseful they might become when the inadvertent harm they cause to a loved one reveals to them how wrong their quest for vengeance was.

However: Under certain circumstances, it might be appropriate to file a lawsuit. Under the Super-Disabilities Act of 1992, superorganizations may not discriminate on the basis of physical handicaps that have caused you to develop other uncanny abilities in compensation. Additionally, discrimination is forbidden on the basis of race, ethnicity, alien origin, religion (your own or that of those who worship the ancient pantheon of which you are a part), sexual orientation, or milquetoastness of secret identity.

Team Tactics

You will soon discover that joint crimefighting brings with it myriad complex tactical issues.

First is the question of organization. In the 1960s, the GLORIOUS PEOPLE'S CRIMEFIGHTING COLLECTIVE FOR SOCIALIST HONOR proved that a communal, hierarchy-free structure could be surprisingly effective in keeping crime off the streets of East Berlin. However, it is worth noting that most of its enemies (such as the GLORIOUS PEOPLE'S CRIME-COMMITTING COLLECTIVE FOR SOCIALIST HONOR) were organized on similar principles. Battles could stretch for days while each side engaged in endless internal debates on whether Marxist-Leninist principles demanded that the first punch come from the efficacious SEVEN YEAR PLAN or the uncannily equal COMRADE CITIZEN. After the fall of the Wall, it became clear that the GPCFCFSH could not compete with more effective West German heroes, and their rallying cry of "From each according to his superpower! To each according to his superneeds!" became but the stuff of history books.

Most modern teams, therefore, vest authority in a single leader. Authority might be permanently granted to a team member based on his or her intellect or seniority, or it might rotate among members. Whatever principle your team chooses, make sure it is agreed upon well in advance. Your foes are unlikely to halt the battle while you consult your bylaws (unless, of course, you are fighting the surprisingly courteous ROBERT'S RULES OF DISORDER).

Once chosen, your leader will need to quickly assess each crimefighting situation, then determine how your individual abilities can best be used in the implementation of justice. This requires the intelligence of a sophisticated manager. Indeed, it is no coincidence that more team leaders have graduate degrees in business administration than in any other field. In recognition of this fact, the famed Educational Testing Service of Solitude has added a Superhero Leadership Aptitude Section to its standard business school exam. A few sample questions will suggest the various challenges of managing a modern team of costumed crusaders.

QUESTION 1 (EASY): THE PYROMANIAC has set fire to an orphanage full of children. Assign each of the following heroes to an appropriate action.

A. THE HOSEMASTER	**1.** Arrest THE PYROMANIAC
B. THE CLOWN PRINCE	**2.** Extinguish the fire
C. THE FIRE MARTIAN	**3.** Comfort the orphans

QUESTION 2 (MEDIUM): On alternating days, THE BIPOLAR OPPOSITE will fight either the most powerful villains or the weakest ones. THE DOLL

COLLECTOR can fight all villains who have toy-related names, and no others. However, due to unresolved sexual tensions within your group, when THE BIPOLAR OPPOSITE feels ineffectual, THE DOLL COLLECTOR prefers to take on villains linked to boys' toys, and contrariwise, when THE BIPOLAR OPPOSITE is brimming with confidence, THE DOLL COLLECTOR would rather battle villains linked to girls' toys. DR. DISTINCTOR will not fight villains whom any human superhero in the area is capable of battling. As THE MER-MAID, you will clean up by fighting whomever is left when the dust settles. Exactly one week after THE BIPOLAR OPPOSITE managed to defeat the previously undefeated TERRIFYING TOWER OF TITANIUM, your team is on patrol, and you come across the following collection of evildoers: VANDOR: THE INDESTRUCTIBLE LASER-BEAM SHOOTING GIANT WITH RAZOR-TIPPED FINGERS; GI JOE STALIN; THE MILDLY IRATE DOLPHIN; and CLAWS BARBIE. Which hero do you assign to each villain?

QUESTION 3 (HARD): If CAPTAIN KETTLE fought
LIZARD-BREATH, who would win?

Rallying Cries

Except for the occasional skirmish in The Silent Zone,
The Eternal Vacuum of Dimension X, or the Library of
Congress, battles will be noisy, chaotic affairs. You
will often find your teammates scattered across the
field of conflict and will need to summon them to a
single place. Since it can be difficult to clip a cell
phone to a costume that consists of a single
formfitting sheet of Spandex, most teams rely on
rallying cries—exclamations, interjections, or pithy
phrases that serve both tactical and inspirational
purposes. Here are some examples to help you and
your teammates choose your own.

Team Name	Good Rallying Cry	Poor Rallying Cry
THE PUZZLE PIECES	PUZZLE PIECES, assemble!	Yo! PUZZLE PIECES! A little help over here!
THE LONDON UNDERGROUND	From Hyde Park Corner to King's Cross–St. Pancras— let justice be served!	Taxi!
THE HIP-HOP HEROES	Take the H to the O / to the P—don't be slow! Take the hip to the hop / to the top of the pops! When the cops can't stop / some zero's tricks, the HIP-HOP HEROES / will funk the fix!	PUZZLE PIECES, assemble!

Team Dynamics

You and your teammates will be spending long hours together in situations ranging from the most casual and relaxing to the most intense and dangerous. It is only natural that you will develop strong affection for some, and deep antipathy for others.

This tendency is exacerbated by the fact that the personalities involved will, by their nature, tend toward the extreme. If, in your civilian life, a friendly smile from an attractive coworker in the midst of a somewhat unnerving performance review has led to an office crush, you can only imagine the feelings that will be stirred by the triumphant embrace of a Spandex-clad specimen of physical perfection after a near-death experience.

These feelings are all perfectly normal and, when dealt with in the forthright manner that all superheroes ought to cultivate, can only result in your team's becoming stronger. However, emotional attachments to supervillains ought to be avoided at all costs. MR. MIRAGE might be able to change his appearance in the blink of an eye, but not even your love will ever change *him*.

CHAPTER EIGHT

MAKING ENEMIES

Science tells us that milk goes bad because of the growth (slowed, but not stopped, by refrigeration) of bacteria (reduced, but not eliminated, by pasteurization). But what makes a person go bad? What combination of malnutrition, miseducation, unsatisfactory job performance evaluations, and social isolation (or full-fledged religious excommunication) warps a person so tortuously that he or she would rather kidnap and hold for ransom a prominent daily newspaper editor's astronaut son than play with a puppy? It does not matter. Something makes baddies bad, but something else confronts them, disarms them, pummels and apprehends them, and that something else is you.

A Glossary of Bad (Abridged)

ARCH-. A prefix meaning "first" or "chief," as in *archbishop*, *archduke*, and *archenemy*. "Arch" as a word in its own right can mean "cunning," "sly," or "roguish," as well as "a curved structure resting on supports at both extremities." Therefore, THE CONSTRUCTED MEMORY has an archenemy in THE NATIONAL ARCHIVIST, but he also has an archenemy in GOLDEN ARCHITECT (OF DESTRUCTION), and an arch arch-archenemy in SARCASTO: MASTER OF GOTHIC CATHEDRAL DEMOLITION.

BAD GUY (sometimes **BADDIE**). One who is depraved, corrupt, base, sinful, atrocious,

The Government Manual for New Superheroes

lacking in moral qualities, ill-natured, ill-willed, vicious, and reprehensible.

CRIMINAL. A bad guy who breaks the law.

ENEMY. One who stands in diametric opposition to another and whose *raison d'être* is to challenge that other's beliefs, ethics, et cetera. Good guys and bad guys are enemies.

EVILDOER. A bad guy who harms women and/or children.

NE'ER-DO-WELL. One who is not good even at being bad.

NEMESIS. Like enemy, but often used to refer to one's *only* enemy (pl. **NEMESES**).

ROBBER. Not the concern of a superhero. Robbers are best left to cops.

VILLAIN. A scoundrel; an inhabitant of a village.

Starting Small

When you begin your superhero career, you might legitimately and without fear of serious ridicule engage only the merest supernumeraries of the true-crime picture—the nameless, interchangeable, indistinguishable, inconsequential hoods and lowlifes who knock over bodegas and pawnshops, who snatch purses and fanny packs, and who play dice in alleys, lean against telephone poles, or loiter in other unwholesome ways. Sooner or later, though, you will have to make enemies fit for a superhero: superbaddies with not just names and costumes, but also big plans and real staying power.

It would be too easy to suggest that making enemies is just like taking a sidekick or enlisting teammates, only with your priorities turned upside down. Nonetheless, the process is similar: Your rivals will be the supervillains who hate what you love, seek to destroy what you strive to protect, and deride what you desire—or who live in your neighborhood and have names or costume colors that are opposite to yours.

Choosing Your Particular Enemies

If you will be the only superhero protecting a certain area—be it defined by natural geography, political boundaries, or fertility of the soil—then you will necessarily if unenviably have a monopoly on the supervillains in residence. That is, every one of them will be your problem. If instead you will be one of two or more superheroes in a region, then it will be in your best interest to oppose chiefly those supervillains whom your particular skill set and equipment best suit you to take on.

If you are a detective-type superhero, then you will find most rewarding tracking, trailing, and outwitting the sneakier, snarkier supervillains. This is why the legendary HARDBOILED DICK spent his days and nights chasing THE SKIRT, hitting THE BOTTLE, taking THE FALL, playing THE SAP, carting THE PATSY off to The Hoosegow of Justice, pounding THE BEAT, seeking THE MALTESE FALCON, shaking THE TAIL, and following THE INTUITION.

Likewise, if you are equipment-oriented, you will no doubt take the most pleasure in engaging like-minded adversaries. His autobiography revealed that GREASE MONKEY preferred tackling the likes of PLANNED OBSOLESCENCE, CLINK AND CLANK, and OVERPRICED MECHANIC.

Identifying Your Nemesis

More likely than not, your nemesis will emerge from the pool of enemies with whom you will have already had numerous encounters, leaving behind the others and rising to the occasion, establishing himself or herself as your most serious adversary, your most dangerous foe, your most dedicated rival. But your nemesis could, in the alternative, be a late entry—this will happen when your nemesis is born of something you will have done: unintentionally dropping him in acid, for example; unwittingly making her lose all of her hair; or inadvertently exposing him as a professional fraud *and* leaving a psychotic alien symbiont that hates you where he might step in it.

Wooing Your Nemesis from Another Superhero

In the best-case scenario, you and your future nemesis will begin your careers at roughly the same time, ensuring that your respective levels of experience will always remain on a par. Eventually, you will become aware of each other and enter into an unspoken, but no less solemn, adversarial relationship.

Less ideal is that your destined nemesis is already linked to another superhero. This is when things can get sticky. If you find yourself in the unenviable position of having to steal another superhero's nemesis, you will want to keep the following in mind:

First, do not assume that the other superhero is as attached to his or her nemesis as it might seem. *Talk to the other superhero.* You just might learn that no feelings are in fact at risk of being bruised.

If, however, the other superhero is attached to his or her nemesis, remember that all is fair in love and war, and this is both—love of justice, and war on crime.

When you have decided to woo another's archenemy, focus your attention on the baddie, and make sure he or she knows from the start that you are interested in having a committed adversarial relationship. Listen carefully when he talks about his plans for world domination; notice and comment when she adds deadly accessories to her costume.

Finally: Although you will already feel that you and your intended have much in common, you might want to make small changes to your own superhero persona to become even more antithetical to the villain you want to make your principal rival. If you are, for example, THE BEETLE, and you wish to impress THE APHID, consider becoming the more specific LADY

BEETLE and thereby indicating your commitment by alluding to the way things are in nature.

Where to Meet a Nemesis (and What to Say)

Government-sponsored studies performed under exacting conditions revealed the following results, which were later exposed to rigorous scrutiny and then revised to conform with generally accepted principles: The best places to meet archenemies include the library, the grocery store, the mall, the park, and your local legislature.

Any superhero who has tried knows that it is not easy meeting—and talking to!—evildoers. It is an awkward adventure every time, no matter how often you have mustered the courage to approach a candidate for enmity and broken the proverbial ice with your muscular, gloved fist. Should you just say,

"Hello," or should you use a line, such as the chestnut that begins, "Is your father a thief . . . ," and ends, " . . . and what kind of thief are you?" with some filler in between about the stars in the sky, et cetera.

Certain lines, moreover, are better received than others. These include:

"Nice shoes. Wanna fight?"

"Did it hurt? When you fell from the heavenly roof of the Skyscraper of Doom?"

"I seem to have lost the number to my Red Phone. Can I have yours?"

"That's a nice shirt. I bet I can talk you out of it, and into a suit of armored tentacles."

Ending It

For better or worse, there comes a time in every adversarial relationship when the antagonism declines, the bad feeling turns to neutral, or to good, and you and your nemesis look one another in the eyeslit only to wonder, *What did we ever hate in each other?* Maybe you will have grown apart, or maybe you will have grown closer, less opposite. Maybe one of you will have decided to hang up the cape, doff the cowl, take off the gloves, throw in the towel. If it is your nemesis who is withdrawing, be gracious in victory. If it is you who has decided to leave the bloody battlefield for greener pastures, then know that our thoughts go with you, superhero.

Afterword

by THE EVILIMINATOR: ELIMINATOR OF EVIL THINGS BUT DEFENDER OF GOOD ONES

When the Government asked for my opinion of an early draft of this handbook, I said that I thought it was missing just a few things. I was assured that future editions would include chapters on the all-important topics of "Bashing Unrighteous Faces," "Mangling the Malignant," and "Snapping the Limbs of Crime." In the meantime, I want to say a few brief words about one of my other favorite topics: gaining superpowers.

Right now, when you're just starting out, you're probably too busy with other worries to ask yourself, "How can I gain the strength of a thousand rhinos?"—unless, of course, you're some kind of troublemaking, question-asking pinko hippie egghead. But after several years of knuckle-punching evildoers, you're going to realize that being able to yank a streetlamp from its concrete base and swing it like a baseball bat will let you send more scum to the hospital and/or morgue than ever before.

Of course, the easiest way to get superpowers is to be born on an alien planet, or in the lost city of Atlantis, or maybe in the floating hall where dwell the mighty gods of some yammering foreigners. But if you did that, you wouldn't have been born into the American way, and you'd have to settle for defending secondary virtues like truth and justice.

So if you want superpowers, you're probably going to have to get them some time after birth. One common technique is to devote yourself to pushing the frontiers of human knowledge into areas where man was never meant to tread in the hopes that an experiment will go horribly awry and you'll end up with the ability to shoot laser beams out of both ears.

This is a great method if you're an egghead. For the rest of us, though, there's only one way to go: *get nuked.*

Scientists used to think the side effects of radiation included vomiting, hair loss, and an increased short-term risk of cancer. Also, death. We now know that the effects of radiation are much more likely to include the power of invisibility, or the proportional strength and speed of a spider, or, at worst, a tendency to transform into a hulking, all-powerful man-beast in times of emotional stress. All in all, it's surprising that more people don't hang out at military test sites, playing their harmonicas, awaiting the sweet, life-improving kiss of a twenty-megaton nuclear explosion.

Sadly, for some reason, most people who sneak into nuclear test sites nowadays are hardcore pacifists. Having enough strength in your little finger to crush a watermelon into a pulp is completely wasted on these troublemaking, question-asking pinko hippies. They're more likely to use such power to make their pinko hippie organic fruit smoothies without a blender than to pop the skulls of evildoers.

Fortunately, if you've gotten through *The Government Manual for New Superheroes* without dissolving into a terrified puddle of wussified goo, then you're clearly made of sterner stuff. So get psyched, get nuked, and get bashing!

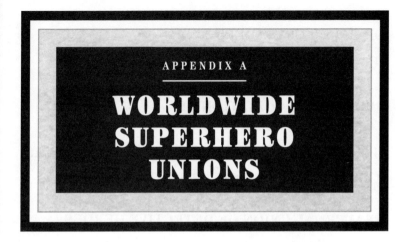

WORLDWIDE SUPERHERO UNIONS

Even superheroes—lone crusaders and team members alike—benefit from membership in groups expressly organized to protect their special interests. Consider joining one of these:

UNITED FEDERATION OF ARCHETYPES

"The oldest superhero union, represents the oldest superheroes, jealously safeguarding their interests in the most oft-imitated character features and facets."

BENEFICIAL ORGANIZATION OF CAPED CRUSADERS

"Boasts a single prerequisite to membership!"

PROTECTIVE COALITION OF CONVERTED VILLAINS

"Lobbies for the equal treatment of those who traded a life of crime for a life of crimefighting."

FRATERNAL UNION OF DETECTIVE HEROES

"Among other benefits, provides economic assistance by periodically purchasing magnifying glasses, prints-dusters, and mini-microphones in bulk."

RIGHTS ALLIANCE OF EXTRATERRESTRIAL CHAMPIONS

"Being from another planet is difficult enough. Being alien and godlike is a full-time job. We can help."

INTERNATIONAL BROTHERHOOD OF FEMALE PARAGONS

"We know that it's not the tight costume, but rather what's under the tight costume, that's important."

BENEVOLENT ORDER OF FIST-FIGHTERS

"Extends an open hand to prospective members; won't knuckle under when bargaining for benefits."

ORGANIZING BOARD OF JOURNEYMEN AVENGERS

"OBJA represents apprentice practitioners of the fine art of superheroic vengeance, because *Vengeance is a minefield.*"

FEDERATED SOCIETY OF MUTANTS AND ALTERED HUMANS

"We fight to change the system so you won't have to change (again)."

AMALGAMATED COMMITTEE OF RADIOACTIVE PERSONS

"A welcoming home for the zapped, nuked, and fried alike."

LABOR ASSOCIATION OF SIDEKICKS, MASCOTS, AND MECHANICS

"Looking out for the underlings, the underdogs, and the grease monkeys."

PLANETARY COUNCIL OF USERS OF ENCHANTED ARTIFACTS

"By the Power of organization for the purpose of negotiation on matters of wages, seniority, working conditions, fringe benefits, and the like . . . we have the Power!"

OTHER PUBLICATIONS AVAILABLE

AT YOUR LOCAL BOOKSTORE:

Heather's Mommy Has Two Identities: A Guide for Children of Crimefighters

So You've Been Bitten by a Radioactive Animal Whose Inherent Abilities Have Been Transferred to You: What Next?

Reverend Revenge's Guide to Retroactive Continuity: How to Revise Your Origins Without Anybody Noticing, by Rabbi Revenge.

Who Moved the Piece of Cheese That Is the Only Substance on Earth That Can Sap My Superpowers?

"I'm OK, You're Evil—But I'm OK with That": Daily Affirmations for Superheroes Who Do Too Much

FREE FROM THE BUREAU OF SUPERHEROICS, BOX 1075, PUEBLO, COLORADO:

Righteous Down to the Seams: Making Sure Your Costume Provider Is Sweatshop-Free

What You Need to Know Before Fighting Crime Abroad

What You Need to Know Before Fighting Crime in Outer Space

What You Need to Know Before Fighting Crime in a Vast Cavern in the Center of the Earth Where Monstrous Bats Breathe Fire

Can I Claim My Sidekick as a Dependent? And 99 Other Common Tax Questions

Buying a Used Hall of Justice—Know Your Rights

Sample
Registration Form

SUPERHERO NAME: _____

I. Identification Data

❒ Human   ❒ Altered Human
❒ Mutant   ❒ Alien

Name: _____
      First   *Middle*   *Last*   *Suffix*

Date of birth: _____ Date of origin: _____

Base of operations: _____
(include ZIP Code) _____
                   _____

    Red Phone/fax no.:(__) __-_____

OFFICE USE ONLY

Name available?

❒ Yes   ❒ No

Hyphen necessary?

❒ Yes   ❒ No

II-A. Costume

Please provide a detailed description of your costume below. Include boot size. Attach additional sheets if necessary.

_____

_____

_____

Cape?　☐ Yes　☐ No

II-B. Insignia

Draw your insignia here:

III. Affiliations

Sidekick?　☐ Yes　☐ No　*If yes, name:* _____

Member of team?　☐ Yes　☐ No　Name of team: _____

Team base at: _____ *of Justice*

Known nemeses *(list in order of first inimical encounter)*:

1. _____　　2. _____

3. _____　　4. _____

5. _____　　6. _____

Names of confidant(e)(s) *(list in order of trustworthiness)*:

1. _____　　2. _____

3. _____　　4. _____

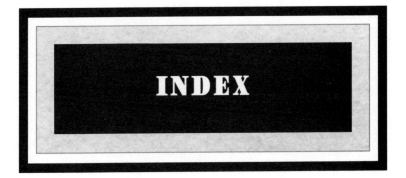

INDEX

ABOUT THE AUTHORS

At the age of one, dressed in a SUPERMAN® costume made by his mother, Matthew David Brozik™ took first prize (a dollar) in a costume contest. Some years later, pretending to be the INCREDIBLE HULK®, he hurled a chair through his bedroom window. He was not punished. As an undergraduate, Matthew studied creative writing with certain literary luminaries and even won some grant money (more than a dollar) to allow him to research the remaining

Catskill Mountains resorts for a novella and a play (neither of which turned out very well at all). He performed on stage as a member of Princeton University's riotous and renowned improvisational comedy troupe *Quipfire!*, which he had cofounded in 1991. His senior thesis was a literary-critical exposition of the *Star Wars* saga. While in law school, he performed stand-up comedy on occasion. (Okay, twice.) His short, quirky fiction has appeared in such publications as the *Sycamore Review*, *Spout Magazine*, *Sidewalks*, *Barbaric Yawp*, the *Palo Alto Review*, and the *Dogwood Journal*. Matthew lives in New York. He is mysteriously single and has no pets.

Photo: NATALIA SIMONS

Jacob Sager Weinstein is absolutely, positively not the supervillain known as THE NOSTRIL, despite what those meddling newspapers keep printing. Instead, he is a former staff writer for HBO's multiple-Emmy-winning *Dennis Miller Live*, and a contributor to *The Onion*. He recently sold a pilot script for a comedy series called *Hangcliff Abbey* to the BBC, and surely the BBC wouldn't participate in the schemes of some sort of universe-destroying madman, would it? His work has also appeared in *McSweeney's* and *Washingtonian Magazine*. He is mysteriously married and has no pets. He lives in London with his wife, Lauren, who is absolutely, positively not the beautiful superhero THE SECOND SOPRANO, whose uncanny powers are the only thing stopping THE NOSTRIL from destroying the universe. Now move along, Earthling.

Photo: LAUREN SAGER WEINSTEIN